Sacred Seasonings

Ideas for Enhancing the Flavor of Your Worship

By

Sherri Purdom

Copyright © 2003 by Sherri Purdom

Sacred Seasonings
by Sherri Purdom

Printed in the United States of America

ISBN 1-591606-01-2

All rights reserved. No part of this publication may be reproduced or transmitted in any form or by any means without written permission of the publisher.

Unless otherwise indicated, Bible quotations are taken from HOLY BIBLE, NEW INTERNATIONAL VERSION®. Copyright © 1973, 1978, 1984 by International Bible Society. Used by permission of Zondervan Publishing House.

The "NIV" and "New International Version" trademarks are registered in the United States Patent and Trademark Office by International Bible Society. Use of either trademark requires the permission of International Bible Society.

Xulon Press
www.XulonPress.com

Xulon Press books are available in bookstores everywhere, and on the Web at www.XulonPress.com.

Acknowledgements

I have been blessed to have many people put in my life to encourage me along the journey of writing this book. Without their laughter, prayers, questions, and sometimes goading, I am not sure I would have listened as hard to the promptings of the Spirit. I give thanks to God for the gift of their presence.

Thank you Terrie Jackson for hearing the first cries of the birthing process and keeping me accountable. Thank you Donice Heriford for helping me see my gifts and how I can use them for God. The two of you saw something in me I didn't even know was there.

Thank you to my reunion group, Karen, Beth, Vicky, and Sherry. You spent many Wednesday nights listening to frustrations and joys. Thank you for trying some of the recipes from the very beginning and sharing with me the experience.

Thank you Thelma, Christi, Karen, and Kathi. Early on, you never let me think this was a crazy idea and helped in trying some things out.

Thank you to my Camino sisters. All of you bless me with a community that continually shows me grace and love. The seeds of this book started in sharing my time and talents with you.

Thank you to my Academy community, especially my covenant group. For the space to be creative and the grace in which you allow me to share with you all, I am truly grateful.

Thank you to my Companions group. Pat, Terre, Ron, Ivan, Raegene, and Peggy, I learn so much from all of you. Thank you for your final input on the recipes and in the editing process.

Most of all thank you to my family. Sarah, Eli, and Rees, you are the best kids in the world. I pray that you continue to be creative in your own ways and follow your dreams. Dan, I could not have completed this without your support, encouragement, and love.

For Mom

Table of Contents

Introduction 11

Gathering Your Ingredients 13

Recipes:
    Play Dough 17
    Stained Glass Candy 21
    Ocean Waves..25
    God's Eyes 29
    Leaf Rubbings..33
    Papier-Mâché Masks..37
    Cinnamon Cutouts 43
    Unleavened Griddle Baked Pita Bread 47
    Snow Globes 51
    Rain Sticks 55
    Peanut Butter and Honey Bees 59
    Pretzels 63
    Musical Instruments 67

Continuing to Feast on the Goodness of the Lord 71

Introduction

My family and friends often laugh at me and say I am unable to follow a recipe or directions for a project as they are written. I am always adding something, changing an ingredient to what I have on hand or comparing several versions to come up with my own. One friend goes as far as to call me a non-conformist! I think of it as developing my own personal style.

I've learned in the last few years, this also applies to my spiritual life. I enjoy trying new things and learning from many different sources. Sometimes the end result is something I want to continue, and other times it gets filed under, "It was a good *idea*." The point is: I'm willing to try. Being open to new ideas and new ways of doing things doesn't mean I am rejecting the traditional. To be able to grow, one must start with a strong basis. I'm just adding a pinch of something new to add flavor or enhance what is already there.

Worship experiences are personal. It is time between you and God. But worship isn't just an hour during the week to sit and listen to how you should be living the Christian life. (Yes, there are times for that too.) Worship is participatory. It is a chance to use all your senses and experience the actual presence of God. It is time to be open the Holy Spirit alive within and perhaps speaking to you. Have you ever been in a worship service and thought you could *feel* God right there beside you?

There are many books out there that can teach you a myriad of ways to commune with God in nature, in prayer, in meditation, in song, in retreat, in devotions, in teaching – the list is endless. All giving you guides to growing in your personal relationship with God. I must confess I have many of these books on my own bookshelves. They have helped me grow in many ways.

This book will be a bit different. It isn't a how-to. Although it will have suggestions for actual things to do. It isn't deep theology. Although you will be asking yourself what things mean to you and how you perceive different symbols of faith. It isn't denominational. Although I do use my United Methodist heritage as my basis, I borrow from other faith traditions. These recipes are written as guided meditations. They can be done alone, but I suggest you try them a small group study or an organized Sunday School class. You will be asked to reflect on things personally, but there are also questions for reflection that can only be enhanced by discussing them with others. Sharing your stories with each other will give you a chance to see how the Holy Spirit is alive and working in others. You might even learn to perceive God in a new way!

Many people will say they do not have a creative bone in their body. I say it doesn't matter. If you want to experience worship as a time with God, look at the everyday items in your life and consider them sacred. Gather them together as they inspire you and let God speak to you through them. My prayer for you is to use this book as a jumping off point for your own ideas. Step out in faith. Try looking at traditional symbols in a new way or in juxtaposition to something out of the ordinary. That simple act may make you stop and think about what you really believe and about the God that makes all things possible.

Gathering Your Ingredients

"No matter where I serve my guests, they always seem to like my kitchen best."
plaque in my mother's kitchen

The kitchen is the hub of a busy household. I have many happy memories sitting around the kitchen table eating or helping my mother create a meal.

As any cook knows, before a dish is created, it has some basic ingredients that get everything started. If it is a soup it is usually a stock of some sort. For a sauce, a roux invites the flavors to join it. And for breads, flour waits patiently in a bowl for yeast or just the right mix of nuts, fruits, and spices. The same can be said of a worship service.

Before anything can be added, one must start with the Word. Obviously, in the context of praising and worshiping God, we need to know just what is the setting. It might be a specific "feast day" or a day set aside by your denomination to celebrate a certain aspect of the church year. Many of these have a service already designed and can be found in some church hymnals or other orders for worship. These services often include scripture, litanies, musical suggestions and prayers. There are many other reference materials that can also give alternative ideas. Each starts in some part with a scripture that brings into focus the theme of that particular celebration.

There are many different translations of the Bible. Some are more appropriate for a particular service than others. A more formal service might rely more on the King James' version than a contemporary service that is using the Living Bible. Get several different versions and compare. The main idea will probably be the same, but the language used can make a big difference to the listener.

The next basic ingredient I use is a concordance. They are invaluable for looking up companion verses and can help you narrow a theme. (Or enlarge it if your imagination is working!) I also rely on Bible dictionaries when a particular word keeps coming up in scripture, but I'm not sure if that is where I want to focus the attention.

Tangible things gathered for nearly all worship services include a table or altar, candles, a cross. The table/altar will be placed in the center of the area to bring focus for the worship experience. The candles invite the presence of the Holy Spirit. And of course the cross reminds us of the one who brings us together. Fabric may also be used to go on the altar, either draped as part of the visual background or as a parament to signify a particular time in the church calendar. Other things will be added, but they aren't necessarily the basic ingredients.

I suggest you explore various bookstores and find a place to refer to for resources. Step out of your comfort zone. Go beyond your own denomination and look other places. You may be surprised at what you may find. Be open to the possibilities that other people who don't have the exact same beliefs you do, will have just the right book or cross or figurine that can help you grow in your relationship with God.

Look in closets, basements, attics, and drawers for things that will help you focus on the main theme of your worship. There may be a reason you held onto that stuff for all of these years. Not all "pack rat mentality" is bad. That old piece of costume jewelry you still have from high school may be just the item you need to focus on for a meditation on giving up possessions to follow Christ. A child's drawing saved in a school box can be a focal point for

Sacred Seasonings

exploring our own creative gifts and talents or remembering the simplicity of God's message of grace and love.

Old magazines are a wonderful source for pictures for collages and displays. Instead of just throwing them out into a recycling bin, take a few minutes and cut out pictures that speak to you. I suggest you get several folders or an expandable file to collect your pictures. The images you gather may be something humorous or questioning, or perhaps the beauty of the scene is what spoke to you. Cut out phrases in headlines. These can make a powerful image with some of the pictures you have gathered. Don't be afraid to put together a picture and a phrase that a first glance may seem incongruous. The whole idea is to see things in a different way. Let your prayers be formed by the thoughts and feelings generated.

The use of crafts gives your listeners something small they can take home to reflect on later. If you yourself are not "crafty", then perhaps you can enlist the aid of friend. Who knows? You may be enabling someone to use a gift or a talent that has been hidden. An item for reflection doesn't have to be anything large. It could be a simple pin made with a silk flower and hot glued to a pin back. It might be a picture from a magazine glued to note card. It could be a couple of sticks tied together with yarn in the form of a cross. Maybe it is a stone. Use whatever you think will express the idea and help your listeners to meditate upon later.

I am forever saving bulletins, programs and newsletters that contain a piece of poetry, a prayer, or a litany that would fit in with something else I am doing. Be sure to always give credit to the author and be mindful of copyright laws. Many things can be used during a worship service or a Bible study, but printing for publication is another matter altogether.

Now that your ingredients are gathered, let's create some food for thought.

Play Dough

"Yet, O Lord, you are our Father. We are the clay, you are the potter; we are the work of your hands."

Isaiah 64:8

Ingredients:

    1 cup all-purpose flour
    1 tablespoon oil
    1 cup water
    1/2 cup salt
    2 teaspoons cream of tartar
    food coloring of your choice

Combine all the ingredients in a medium sized pot. (Don't forget you can mix colors to create new ones!) Stir with a wooden spoon constantly over medium heat. The mixture will stay liquid at first and then, all of a sudden, it will come together into a mass. Keep stirring until all the dough comes together. Remove from heat immediately.

    Turn the dough out onto the counter. When it is cool enough to handle, knead it for a few minutes. Once it has a nice, silky texture, the play dough is ready to use. The play dough can be stored in a sealed plastic bag in the refrigerator for several months.

Nearly every person I know has at one time or another, played with modeling clay or play dough. The scent of the store bought brand is one of the most recognizable odors around. Ask any adult to name common childhood activities, and play dough will almost always come to mind.

Give each person a clump of dough. Let them roll it around in their hands for a few minutes. If it is has just come out of the refrigerator it may be cool to the touch and perhaps a bit stiff. Notice how the longer you handle it, the easier it moves and the warmer it becomes.

Start by making a ball between you hands. Do you move your hands quickly or deliberately? Is your ball smooth or does it have small lines in it? Now move to making a cylinder. Once again you roll it between your hands, but this time the movement is a bit different. Can you make your cylinder even? What happens when you push from either or both ends?

Flatten the play dough out. How much pressure did you have to exert? Did you do it between your palms or did you use the tabletop? Keep pulling and stretching, making the dough flatter and flatter. Does the color of the dough change slightly as it gets thinner? Continue pulling until the dough begins to tear apart. Where did it start to tear? Did it start in the middle or near an edge? Did it tear in several different places simultaneously? Now fold the dough over itself. Press it together. Can you tell where it tore apart before?

Reflect upon the dough as a symbol of you. Sometimes we feel "cold" and our prayer lives are stiff from inactivity. When we allow God to begin moving us, we grow warmer and more pliable. We begin to feel God shaping us. Sometimes we feel our shapes happen to quickly and we aren't strong enough to withstand the pulling. We feel as though we have hollow spots or that we have been stretched too far and we can't seem to remain whole. God in his wisdom knows our weaknesses. He folds us over to rework us. And as soon as he begins again in us, we can no longer see where the hurt was before. All of this is done so deftly and simply. The more we resist the work of the creator, there is more of a chance for us to develop empty spots. But when we relinquish control and allow ourselves to be shaped into what God wants us to be, the easier we move. We may think we know what God is making of us, but sometimes the final outcome doesn't come from the beginning moldings.

Begin shaping your dough into a form. Let your imagination run wild. Don't be afraid to divide the small piece of dough you have to create something with several parts. Forget that you are an adult. What you are bringing into existence doesn't have to be a great work of art. Remember as a child, no matter what your drawing may have looked like, your parents told you how beautiful it was?

Some in the group will probably form a dish or a cup. Reflect on the idea of being vessels for God. Is your dish to bring offerings to God? Does your cup "runneth over" with blessings given to you by your creator? If you imagine your cup to be empty, how will you fill it?

Someone else may shape an animal form. Why did they make that one? Does it represent a pet or a particular interest the person has?

Maybe your creation is a freeform work of art. Perhaps it is something that will make you smile or help you meditate on a particular idea. It may be lifelike or abstract. Whatever the outcome of the time spent modeling your clay, it is born of you. And it is born of the one who created you.

It is important to remember that to become permanent, clay must be fired at extremely hot temperatures. While we do not fire this particular type of clay, it can be left out in the open to air dry for a couple of days. Once a piece has been dried (either by firing or air drying) we handle them differently. No longer do we push and pull to form something, but rather we carry it gently so as to not break our creation. And sometimes we will see that after all the work, we may have developed small cracks. Just because something doesn't come out the way you envisioned, doesn't mean it isn't worth keeping or using. Even a bowl with a crack in it can be used to hold fresh fruit on a table. There was a popular phrase in the '70's, "God doesn't make junk." He uses us as we are and tries to mold us into what he has envisioned for us. Let Him do the work.

Questions for reflection:

1. When was the last time you felt God shaping you into a new creature?
2. How did you feel as you were pulled and stretched? Was this growth? Did you realize what was happening to you? Did you resist or try to form yourself?
3. When given the chance to create something yourself, did you feel you were unable to think of what exactly to do? How did you let go of the "adult" in you and become a child again?
4. Share with others the shape you formed. Why did you created that? Because it was easy? Were you afraid of what others in the group may think of you? Would you be willing to allow this shape to become permanent? Why or why not?
5. When you see an object, do you automatically look for its useful nature or are you able to see other uses than first intended?

Oh, Creator God, thank you for taking the time to mold us. We so often don't understand the idea you have for us. Help us trust you as you pull and stretch us past what we feel is comfortable. Help us have the courage to be more than what people see at first. May we be useful vessels or beautiful works of art that others may see your work in us. Amen.

When our eyes see our hands doing the work of our hearts, the circle of Creation is completed inside us, the doors of our souls fly open and love steps forth to heal everything in sight.

Michael Bridge

Stained Glass Candy

"For you were once darkness, but now you are light in the Lord. Live as children of light."

Ephesians 5:8

Ingredients:

2 cups sugar
3/4 cup white corn syrup
1 cup water
food coloring
flavoring or oils such as peppermint, cinnamon, lemon, orange, cherry, etc.

Combine sugar, corn syrup and water. Stir just to dissolve sugar. Cook, without stirring, until hard-crack stage is reached or 300 degrees on a candy thermometer. Remove from fire and add food coloring and flavoring as desired. (Just a few drops of each will do.) You may want to divide the candy into different sections and color and flavor them in various ways. Pour into a buttered jellyroll pan. Cool. You may score with the back of a table knife when it begins to cool, and then break into squares or let it harden and then break into irregular pieces.

Nearly every church has at least one stained glass window. Often they are memorials to saints who have sat in the very same pews many years before us. They depict famous stories or persons from the Bible or Christ himself. Sometimes they are just mosaics of color and light that don't represent any one thing, but rather draw us into its patterns and play with our senses.

Stained glass was made long before words were written to describe it. Churches in France and Germany from the 10th century had windows made of stained glass depicting Christ and Biblical scenes. Medieval men "read' the windows as much as experienced them.

The process of making glass itself is an amazing process of taking sand and firing it at intense temperatures to transform it into a molten quality that can be shaped or flattened. Colored glass develops when metallic salts and oxides are added during the process.

We can call to mind many famous stained glass pieces from history. The rose window in the cathedral of Notre Dame is an example of one of the most beautiful works of art made from small bits of glass put together to form one large shape. Tiffany lamps also use many pieces of glass to compose a picture that is made clearer when the light shines through.

Look at the "stained glass" you have made. Take a piece and hold it to the light. Is your piece a defined geometric pattern, or just an irregular shape? Notice how the color is part of the glass. It is not simply a piece of clear or white glass that has been painted. The color is an element of the glass itself. And yet, is the color exactly the same throughout, or does it striate as the light flows through it?

Hold your piece of glass behind a light source. How does the light change the way you view the color? Holding it up to the light you were able to see most all of the colors together. But with the light in front, different pieces sparkle in different ways.

Imagine for a moment you are part of a large stained glass window made up of the people in the room with you. How do you all fit together? What is the solder that holds you together?

Sacred Seasonings

What color are you? What picture do you form? Are some pieces larger than others?

Think about the "fires" you have been through that have transformed you into what you are today. Was it so intense you were made into something else? What was added to you to give you your color today?

Return again to the picture made up of the group's many pieces. Each individual piece is unique, yet the image is not complete if a piece is missing. Where is your light source? Is it behind you illuminating all the pieces at once? Or is it also in front of you, letting each individual detail sparkle in his or her own special way? As the light dances through you or is reflected off of you, can the color be seen on other objects? Even when it seems dark, are you able to recognize the different patterns and various colors?

God is of course our light source. From him we are able to illuminate others to his grace and majesty. From him we are able to show ourselves to be unique and filled with gifts given specifically to us. From him we are able to be a part of a much bigger picture that can only be recognized by backing up a bit and taking it all in together. From him we are able to dance and play and shine on others filling them with laughter and beauty. We truly are Children of Light.

Questions for reflection:

1. What is your favorite stained glass piece? Is it a window or something else? Why do you like it?
2. As a piece of stained glass, are you merely decorative or do you have a function?
3. Do you feel as though you are part of a "bigger picture"? How can you use you personal gifts better to bring focus to the group as a whole?
4. When God's light shines through you, do you feel you are revealing all your various shades of color or just the most brilliant at the moment?
5. Do you shine, reflect, or dance?

Oh God, Light unto our world, thank you for shining through what may seem like clouded glass to show us your splendor. May we shine on others with the gifts and graces you have given us. Help us to remember that even when it seems dark, a small flicker of a candle can illuminate your work in us. Amen.

> People are like stained glass windows; they sparkle and shine when the sun is out; but when the darkness sets in their true beauty is revealed only if there is a light from within.
>
> Elizabeth Kubler-Ross

Ocean Waves

"Mightier than the thunders of many waters, mightier than the waves of the sea, the Lord on high is mighty!"
Psalm 93:4

Ingredients:

    plastic pop bottle (or other small jar) with lid
    water
    baby oil
    food coloring

In plastic bottle, mix equal parts of water and baby oil. Add food coloring as desire. Replace cap or lid. (May be glued shut to prevent a leakage.) Slowly tip bottle back and forth create "waves".

    Cup your hands over your ears. Close your eyes. Hear the roar of the "ocean". Concentrate on your breathing. Feel your chest rise and fall. Notice the ebb and flow of your life. As you continue to sense your breath, focus again on the sound you hear. Does it seem to drown out other noises?

    Pick up your bottle of ocean waves. Hold it to the light and notice the color. Swirl it around and tip it back and forth. Watch the waves crash upon each. Try tipping it even slower. How does this change the force of the waves?

Our own lives are so much like the sea. Our days have a definite ebb and flow to them. We awaken, get ready for our day, go about our business (and busy-ness) and retire for the night. We eat and sleep and bathe in the natural rhythm of our life. God ordered our world to be so. He made us part of this natural realm.

In the rush of our busy lives, we don't notice the order of things. We focus on the crisis at hand or the ongoing whirlwind of activities. We study the details and dissect each individual aspect of what we do looking for imperfections. We seem to be in a constant state of "improving".

Improving, enhancing, perfecting. "How can I make this better?" we ask. Ah, the "I" of it. What about our place in the big picture of life? How can we stay connected to the world if we are only concentrating on our very small piece of it?

Let's go back to our ocean. Notice as you tip it up and the waves begin to roll, how they fall on each other: There is great power in water. Anyone who has stood at the edge of the ocean and felt the undertow, can tell you there is real force in the waves. Imagine standing at the water's edge feeling the sand gently easing you toward the surf. Don't be frightened. We aren't going very far. Imagine the feeling of each wave as it pushes your ankles toward the shore at the same time your feet are being pulled toward the sea. As you stand there, think about all the people who have stood there before you. Look out at the ocean that seems to have no end. But we know there is something out there we can't see. On the other side of the vastness is someone on the other side looking toward you.

God did not make this awesome world flat, but rather circular. It and we are connected always. Many times we think only about what is happening right here, right now. But somewhere on the opposite side of this planet is someone preparing food for the family; tying the shoe of a child; stoking the hand of a loved one; taking time to hear the breathe of life. In this moment, feel the power of the living God.

Questions for reflection:

1. Do you find it difficult to listen to "nothing"? Why?
2. What immediate crisis are you thinking about right now?

Sacred Seasonings

Is it a concern you can actually do something about or are you just worrying about your inability to act?

3. Are you able to be happy with yourself today? Are you focused on improving something about yourself? What exactly? Why?

4. How do you see yourself in God's "big picture"?

5. How do you remember your connectedness daily?

6. Are you aware that God is the "someone" looking back at you? Describe the power of God you see today.

God of wonder and of our world, thank you for this moment in time to remember all of your universe and our very small part in it. In times of doubt and uncertainty, help us to see the power of our own lives on others. As we stand alone facing whatever challenges us, may we know you are always on the other side. Amen.

The deep emotional conviction of the presence of a superior reasoning power, which is revealed in the incomprehensible universe forms my idea of God.

Albert Einstein

God's Eyes

"So it was; and God saw all that he had made and it was very good."

Genesis 1:31

Ingredients:

    2 small fairly smooth sticks about 5 inches in length
    string or yarn

Begin by taking the two sticks and crossing them to form a "+". Start by wrapping the string around the middle of the crossed sticks securing them together, crossing to the left and to the right alternately. Once string is secured, start with the stick going up. Wrap string once around the stick counterclockwise. (Keep string close to the part you have already secured.) Move to the next stick (on the right) wrapping it once counterclockwise. Continue moving around the "+" wrapping once at each stick keeping string tight and close to the previous looping. When the God's Eye is as large as you want to make it, cut string and tie off string securely to stick.

    "Look out!" "Watch here you are going!" "Can't you see I'm in the middle of something?" "What are you looking for?" "I can see you are upset."

Many people will tell you their sense of sight is the most important to them. We all rely on it nearly every minute of every day. And because we use this sense without really thinking about it, let us take a few minutes to reflect on seeing the unseen.

I doubt anyone would tell you they enjoy having someone else look over their shoulder while they are trying to do something. Whether it is reading a newspaper or completing a simple task, we do not like to have our every move monitored. We are appalled at the prying eyes of security cameras that now permeate our daily lives in seemingly private moments.

The thought of having someone constantly watch us makes us nervous or anxious. We perceive another's interest in what we are doing as "just waiting until we mess up." As parents we look at the things our children do in praise and with pride. Moms have long been accused of having eyes in the back of their heads. Most moms I know can see through the walls of two rooms and be able to tell what a child is really doing with that toothbrush or bowl of cereal! Have you ever considered how God watches our every move? There is nothing that we do, no matter how secretive we think we are, that God does not notice. Yet, for some reason, we think that we can get away with a small indiscretion because "no one will know just this once."

God not only sees our every move, but he also sees us in our nakedness. We cannot hide from the all-seeing eye of God. Jonah tried that. It didn't work. When God wants us to do something, he will pursue us until we have completed the task. Just as a parent would, he tries to protect us. He knows the hurts we try to hide deep within ourselves and he wants to make things right again.

If our eyes are "the window to our soul", then we have an opportunity to look into the very being of those around us. How many times have you been able to discern another's emotion just by the look in their eyes? We can see anger in the narrowing of the eye. Laughter in the upturn at the far corner. Excitement when the pupils dilate. Questioning with the lift of the top of the eyebrow. Innocence in wide-eyed expectancy. Passion in a deep unfaltering gaze. Contentment as a calm openness. Panic in the darting of the eyes back and forth. We can also sense another person's character by looking in their eyes: honesty, treachery, and truth. Our perceptions are not infallible of course, but in sizing up a situation, the look in someone else's eyes tells us a great deal.

Are other people able to tell how you are feeling by looking at your eyes? Can your soul be read by seeing into your eyes? Where does your soul reside? I believe it is in our hearts. When we believe something deeply, when we rely on faith, it dwells in our heart. We know deep in our hearts when things are true. God asks us to listen with our heart and he speaks directly to it. In turn, whatever we are feeling is expressed back to the world through our eyes.

What do you see when you gaze at the world? Do you see the problems of the world? Do you see those insurmountable images of despair and pain? Do you look for the good in people? Do you see the needs of others or do you turn a "blind eye" to their problems? Do you search for beauty? Are you always looking for results?

We look for, at, toward, back, into, and beyond. It is a matter of perspective. Perhaps we should try looking at things from God's viewpoint. Imagine a drawing of a roadway. In the foreground, the road is wide and we can clearly make out each line on the pavement. But as the road continues off into the distance, it seems to blend together until finally it is only a single spot in the picture. What if we could see that distant place with the same perspective we of things at our feet?

Look at the God's Eye you made. See how easily it is to separate each strand of string on the outer edges? As you follow the pattern into the center, notice how it becomes harder to make out each single thread, as they become a tight knot in the middle. Feel the difference in texture of the strings in the middle and those on the outer edge. Those on the edge seem looser, more pliable. Even the sticks are still moveable on the outer edges, but are held in place in the center.

Our journey of faith is much like this God's Eye. We begin with a strong foundation that binds us tightly to God and his word. His love is wound around us so that we become strong, yet soft to the touch. As we grow in this faith, we are still bound together in community, but we are also more open to the new paths where God leads us. Hang your God's Eye up so that you may be reminded of the paradox of this all-seeing God who is invisible.

Questions for reflection:

1. Describe a time when you felt someone was looking over your shoulder. What was the outcome? Were you surprised to find out their motive for watching you was not what you thought it was?
2. When you see a group of people gathered together, what do you think is going on? Is it a positive or negative gathering?
3. Have you ever tried to hide an emotion? Were you successful? What is the most difficult emotion for you to hide?
4. Where do you see God? Have you ever tried to hide from him? What did you do?

Heavenly Father, you see us as your children. You see us when we fall down and when we disobey. Yet you continually watch over us even when we try to hide from you. Your love encircles us and binds us together.

Help us to see each other with love. Let us look past the outward appearances and into the hearts of those we meet. Let us be more open to letting others see inside of us. May we remember this is the world you have created and we can see that it is good. Amen.

Discovery consists in seeing what everyone else has seen and thinking what no one else has thought.

Albert Szent-Gyorgoi

Leaf Rubbings

"Before I formed you in the womb I knew you, and before you were born I consecrated you a prophet to the nations."

Jeremiah 1:5

Ingredients:

Various leaves (preferably those that have not dropped from trees yet)
Thin writing paper (not heavy construction paper)
Crayons

Place leaf, lower side up, under a sheet of thin paper. Hold the paper and leaf so they will not move. Use a crayon and rub in the same direction on the paper to get an impression of your leaf.

Every day of our lives we have some sort of relationship to the plants that inhabit our world. Plants exist in every part of the world, from mountains to deserts to oceans. We eat them as food. We use them as shelter in the building of homes. We wear clothing woven from their fibers. Some of us take medications or wear cosmetics extracted from the various parts of the plant. We depend upon plants for the very air we breathe. In some way, each day we come in contact with some form of plant.

Plants are identified by their shape. No two plants are exactly alike. Even among the same species of plants, microscopically a plant can be identified individually by the veins and small hairs it possesses. Each plant has its own "fingerprint" just as you or I.

Just as in our bodies, plants use the veins in its leaves like blood vessels to carry the nutrients that enable the plant to live. The process of photosynthesis is in no small way a miracle of life. The cells of the plant contain a pigment called chlorophyll. It is this chlorophyll that absorbs energy form the sunlight and uses it in transforming carbon dioxide (the gas we exhale as we breath) and water into a type of sugar. The plant uses this sugar as food for energy and growth. In turn, the plant will give off oxygen that we breathe. Scientists have not been able to duplicate this life sustaining process of photosynthesis in the laboratory. How intertwined we are with our world!

As you look at your leaf rubbing, think for a moment how intertwined you are with the little things in your life. How interdependent are you on other people in your life? Who has left an impression on you? What kind of impression do you leave on other people.?

In the same way, we depend on plants to sustain our lives. We rely on other people to nourish and support us. Just as the stalk of a leaf is present to hold the leaf out toward the light, we hold each other out toward the light of God. Sometimes we feel as if pieces of our leaves have been torn off and we are of little use to others. But notches in leaves allow for light to shine on lower leaves of the plant. Other times we may feel we are overshadowing those around us. Perhaps we are only acting as a forest canopy, sheltering the younger plants from the harsh environment.

Can you see the veins of your leaf clearly? Notice how they all come together in the center and the stalk becomes more prominent. Imagine the inner workings of the plant. Try to envision the cells moving up and down along the vein. Think about the life force giving and taking invisible gases that produce so much energy. Think about the supreme life force that breathes life into you. How do you use your energy?

As you colored your impression of your leaf, were you able to keep a steady pressure making the color uniform? Is your rubbing

Sacred Seasonings

full of variations? Did you use only one color? Do you sense texture in the picture of your leaf?

Leaves change as they age. Young leaves are soft and pliable. In midlife, a leaf becomes rougher and more weathered. As leaves become more aged, they become brittle. In this stage they also may change colors and once again capture our attention. Eventually, as they die and fall to the ground, they decompose into humus in the soil that feeds new growth in the plant.

Plants are adaptive to their growing conditions. We have all seen houseplants leaning toward a window to capture more light. Some plants grow protective needles or spines to keep animals at bay. Others produce a poison or a sting to ward off predators. Flowering plants have adapted to attract insects to help the plant distribute pollen. Who hasn't noticed butterflies on flower petals? The water lily adapted its leaves over time to lie flat on the surface of the water. These leaves are held by such strong stalks, they are able to hold the weight of frogs as they sit near the cool water.

We often ponder how closely we are (or are not) related to animals. But do we realize how much in common we have to the simple plants around us? From the dandelion weed to the mighty oak, we are tied to a world in ways only a master designer could have imagined.

Questions for reflection:

1. Who has made the deepest impression on you? Do you see this in a positive or negative way?
2. Thinking about the imprint made on you as a child, how have you adapted to your "growing conditions"? Do you attract people to you, or have you grown a protective way to keep others from getting too close?
3. How do you nourish those around you? Are you able to receive what they have to give you in return?
4. How prominent is the workings of God in your life? Like the large vein running down the center of a leaf, do you allow God to carry sustenance to you? What nutrients are necessary for you to grow in your spiritual life?

Creator God, we are awed by our small part in your world. Help us to see how we are dependent not only on this world you have given us, but on each other. Give us wisdom to help support those around us and courage to accept their encouragement and love in return. Amen.

He who walks in another's tracks leaves no footprints.
Joan Bannon

Papier-Mâché Masks

"I will give you the treasures of darkness, riches stored in secret places, so that you may know that I am the Lord, the God of Israel, who summons you by name."

Isaiah 45:3

Ingredients:

    Papier-mâché paste (see below)
    Balloon
    Masking tape
    Torn strips of newspaper

To make paste, combine 1/2 cup of all-purpose flour and 2 cups cold water in a bowl. Add that mixture to 2 cups of water boiling in a saucepan and bring to boil again. Stir occasionally. Remove from the heat and stir in 3 tablespoons of sugar. It will thicken as it cools. When it is cool enough to handle, it is ready to use.

1. Blow up balloon to approximately the size of your head.
2. Make a wad of tape into the shape of a nose. Tape this "nose" to the balloon where the nose would be on a face. (Keep in mind, the eyes are actually the midpoint of the face.)

3. Dip a strip of newspaper into the papier-mâché paste. Use your fingers to slide off the excess paste, and affix the strip to the balloon. Repeat, covering one side of the balloon in the shape of a face. Be sure to leave openings for eye holes. Let the strips dry and harden. To strengthen the mask, repeat covering with papier-mâché again.
4. After mask has dried completely, gently peel away from the balloon and masking tape nose. (May be easier if balloon is popped.) Paint as desired.

Masks are deeply rooted in history and culture of many people around the globe. The first masks date back to ancient Greek drama and African tribal rituals and celebrations. Masks are use to conceal, disguise, or function as a pretense for something else. All masks at some point in history represented a symbolic form of deities, spirits, rites of passage, or protection. By using a mask, a person or performer could tell a story, act out a piece of history, and participate in a ritual without the human person underneath being the focus of attention.

Many of these early masks were stylized with exaggerated features so that there would be little confusion to whom the mask represented. One of the most common of these would be the "comedy or tragedy" mask of theatre. If a character wore Comedy, he could not only represent humor, but also tease other characters thereby bringing attention to a situation. The same can be said of Tragedy. He might represent a horrific situation; but could also bring light to the absurdity of melodrama.

Ritual masks have always played a vital role in the religious and cultural aspects of a people. Many cultures believe that spirits inhabit the mask itself, thereby making it a sacred object. When it is being worn, the wearer is believed to have been transformed into or is possessed by the spirit represented in the mask. Some cultures participate in ceremonies asking these spirits for help with their needs, both communal and personal, such as Native American dances for rain and African fertility rituals. Funerary masks were placed on the bodies of the deceased to protect them from evil spirits or to guide the dead person's spirit to the afterlife.

Most of the masks we use today are part of theatre or are used as a utilitarian protection. Clowns wear masks to entertain us. Welder's masks are use to shield the metal worker's eyes, medical masks to prevent the spread of disease, and sports masks are used for protection in baseball, hockey, etc.

Perhaps there is another mask we wear daily but fail to recognize because the face looks like our own. It is the face of understanding when we are confused but don't want to seem ignorant. It is the face of agreement in a group situation when we don't want to be singled out as the only voice of opposition. It is the face of happiness when our hearts are heavy or cold and we don't want anyone else to see our pain. It is the face of wholeness when we are broken.

The Latin word for mask is *persona*. How much of what we show the world is really the person inside? We are all so good at impersonating an image of what we think we should be or what we think others want us to be. We "put up a good front" when things are challenging. We "put on a brave face" when our lives seem out of control. But who are we really? Who are you today?

Masks worn by pre-Lenten revelers during Mardis Gras, seem to give the wearer license to do or say things they might not do or say in their "normal" life. In wearing a mask, the person feels a sense of security that no one will know who they really are. Yet a simple mask is hardly protection. There are other things that may give you away: your voice, your mannerisms, and those people around you with whom you associate. After you have removed your mask, can you really return to your life as if nothing happened?

We all know someone who tries very hard to be someone he is not. They might even have several different masks to wear for different people in different situations. Perhaps they do not intentionally want to deceive others, but unless they are able to show some part of their true self, they are at the very least deceiving themselves.

As you made your mask, did you notice how wet the papier-mâché felt? It was necessary to wipe off excess so that it would adhere properly. Sometimes the paste is warm to the touch and other times it feels cold. Perhaps the strips of newspaper didn't quite stay where you first placed them. What did you do to keep them in place? How hard was it to keep the eyes open? Was it difficult to separate the dry mask from the base? Were you concerned with damaging your new mask as you peeled it away from the balloon? How do you feel when there are cracks in your human mask?

Holding your mask up to your face, does it fit the shape of your head? Can you see out the eye openings? If you are able to see out, is your sight limited? Did you also allow a hole for a mouth? How does it feel not having the freedom to have your voice heard as clearly as you would like?

Taking off our masks is risky business. There is a connection between the outward face and the inward feelings of our heart. We usually don't want others to see the emotions holding the mask to our head. To express them might mean acknowledging them and facing them ourselves. What emotions are holding your mask? Would the perception people have of you be different if they saw the "real you"? Really?

Occasionally, we allow others to see past the various masks we wear. We lower the masks, wash off the makeup, expose ourselves at the risk of the unknown. We often forget God sees not only the outward, visible shell, but straight into our hearts. He sees past anger, hurt, fear—even love—to the very core of what He created. We can never truly hide behind the masks we try to wear.

Questions for reflection:

1. Which type of mask are you most uncomfortable wearing? Theatrical, ritual, celebratory, protective? Why?
2. Look at the mask in your hands. What feelings does it bring to mind? How does it make you feel?
3. If masks can represent spiritual deities, does the mask you wear reflect your image of God? What masks do you wear at feasts and social gatherings? Do you posses an attitude of thanksgiving or petition?

Sacred Seasonings

4. Did you choose to paint or decorate your mask? Explain any symbolism you may have attached to your mask.

5. Trade masks with another person. What does it feel like "in someone else's skin"? How is it different from your own. Are you anxious to trade back?

Oh God, creator of who I am and who I am yet to become, thank you for opportunities to lower my mask. Help me remember my true protection comes from you. Help me have the courage to reveal what is hidden, even at the risk of exposing my imperfections. Amen.

"Who are you?" said the Caterpillar.
Alice replied, rather shyly, "I-I hardly know sir, just at present—at least I know who I was when I got up this morning, but I think I must have changed several times since then."

Alice in Wonderland

Cinnamon Cutouts

"Consequently, you are no longer foreigners and aliens, but fellow citizens with God's people and members of God's household."

Ephesians 2:19

Ingredients:

Cinnamon
Apple sauce

Mix together equal portions of the ingredients. (Do not heat or cook.) The dough should be as thick as cookie dough. Sprinkle additional cinnamon on a work surface. Knead the dough until it becomes little less sticky and you are able to roll it to about a 1/4 inch thickness. Cut out shapes with cookie cutters or templates. (If you want to hang them when they are dry, poke a small hole in each cutout using a straw.) Lay the shapes on waxed paper and let them air dry at room temperature. Turn them over several times a day until they are dry. (It is possible to speed up the drying process by putting them in a very low oven for two hours. But this method sometimes makes them more brittle.)

At holiday time, our homes are usually filled with the aroma of baked goods. The smell of cinnamon wafts through the air and we connect with feelings of "home" and "family". Cinnamon is one of the most common spices known and it is probable that all of us have some in our kitchens.

Cinnamon, for a relatively common spice, is actually much more exotic. It grows as a bushy evergreen and is native to Sri Lanka and eastern India. As a member of the laurel family, it is a distant cousin to the bay leaf and avocados. Branches are cut from the tree and the inner bark is harvested and allowed to dry. As it dries, the bark curls up into the familiar quills we know as cinnamon stick. A similar plant called cassia grows in China. The cassia is stronger and bitterer in taste, but still has the cinnamon flavor and grows much the same way. Cassia is one of the essential spices used in the Chinese Five-Spice mixture.

Cinnamon and cassia found their way to the Middle East at least 2000 years before the Christian era. They probably came with Indonesian traders who sailed long before Western civilization ventured beyond the Mediterranean. Eventually the Arabians became the world's traders. They would make up fantastic stories about where and how the cinnamon was harvested to maintain their monopoly on the trade. These stories would be filled with winged creatures, poisonous snakes, and great feats to harvest this strange, yet familiar spice.

Haven't we all, at one time or another, wished we could embellish our life story to make it seem more appealing? Is there something in your past you would rather keep hidden, so you make up a tale to ward off strangers?

Take a moment to inhale the fragrance of the cinnamon. It is at once sweet and heady. In the book of Exodus (Exodus 30:22-26), the Lord instructs Moses to gather cinnamon with other spices and make a holy ointment to anoint the Ark of the Covenant. A *holy* ointment. Not unlike the frankincense brought to the manager. Or the jar of expensive oil Mary uses with her hair to wash the feet of Jesus. A simple spice used to glorify God.

We often feel as if our lives are not exciting enough. We long to travel or make our mark on the world. We seek success in material things. There is a never-ending quest to "do better", "do more", or "get ahead". Sometimes we spend most of our lives, looking for that one thing we are supposed to do. When we stop, it is usually out of frustration instead of a need to rest. We try to find the answers to all our questions "out there", instead of letting some of the answers come to us. We are always searching, but rarely seeing what is right in front of us.

Cinnamon was once considered more valuable than gold. The ancient Egyptians used it in embalming mixtures and in medieval Europe it was used in religious rites. Cinnamon was one of the first spices to be sought during the explorations of the "new world" in the 15th and 16th-centuries. It was the most profitable spice in the Dutch East India Company trade. Indirectly, it led to the discovery of America.

Where are you going? Is there something you keep seeking? Are you looking for adventure or a new direction? Sometimes the things we imagine to be so exotic and enticing are really common things seen from a different viewpoint. Think about cinnamon in its original form. It is a piece of bark. As you kneaded your dough, did you notice how much the cinnamon felt like dirt or sawdust? How could this be sought after? What was its hidden value? What is your hidden value?

Cinnamon makes us think of cookies and pies and spiced cider. It is one of the first spices we think of in our kitchens. It is used the world over in foods ranging from main dishes to desserts. Cinnamon comes from a foreign, faraway land, yet is at home where we are today.

Questions for reflection:

1. What kinds of things do you associate with cinnamon? Are they memories tied to people in your past?
2. Do you see yourself as exotic or common? Why? Are you happy in that role? How would you change?
3. What is your most prized possession? Is it of monetary value? Would you consider it "more precious than gold"?
4. What do you do to glorify God? In doing so, do you use *things*? Are you able to do it as you go about your life daily, or only on special occasions?

5. How did you dry your cutouts? Were you anxious to get the drying process over? Why is waiting for your "discovery" so difficult to do?
6. Recall a time when you have felt like a stranger. Where were you? How did other people react to you? How did you feel? Did you ever come to feel at home in that situation?

Creator God, you who brings us things from many lands and many peoples, help us to see the glory and worth of our lives right now. Make us aware of the many ways we add spice to the lives of others. May what we do, give you all glory and honor. Amen.

The real voyage of discovery consists not in seeking new landscapes, but in having new eyes.

Marcel Proust

Unleavened Griddle Baked Pita Bread

"Go, eat your bread with gladness and drink your wine with a joyful heart for it is now that God favors what you do."

Ecclesiastes 9:7

Ingredients:

3 cups flour
1 teaspoon salt
1 cup warm water
vegetable oil

Combine flour and salt. Stir in enough water so that the dough pulls away from the sides of the bowl and is no longer sticky. Stir until smooth. Knead on a board for 5 minutes. Divide dough into 12 portions and shape into smooth balls. Cover with a damp cloth or towel. Let rest 5 to 10 minutes. Press each ball flat and roll into a 6" or 7" circle. Cover again with damp towel. Lightly oil a griddle or skillet. Cook until brown and bubbly spots appear on the bottom (about 90 seconds). Turn over and brown the other side. Remove from griddle and wrap immediately to keep warm.

Bread has been a part of the human diet as long as grains have been grown for food. It is so much a part of our daily lives, we barely think about its presence. Imagine going into a bakery and seeing all the different kinds of bread. Crusty loaves of French bread. Italian bread sticks. Russian black bread. Mexican tortillas. Indian nan. Southern cornbread. Scones, tea cakes, muffins. Crackers and biscuits. Maybe even pre-sliced loaves of white bread for sandwiches.

Our memories of childhood often include someone making bread. Perhaps it was a loaf of bread made for a special holiday meal. Or maybe it was a pan of biscuits made for supper every night. Have you ever tasted bread toasted in the oven on cold winter morning to be served with hot oatmeal? Can you smell a loaf of pumpkin bread coming out of the oven?

The earliest bread was unleavened and was made from a mixture of flour and water and then dried in the sun on flat stones. Unleavened simply means it is made without yeast or other ingredients that would cause the dough to rise. Passover and the "Festival of Unleavened Bread" is an eight day celebration symbolizing Israel's flight from Egypt. In their haste to leave as God had commanded through his servant Moses, the Hebrew people took their dough before it had a chance to rise. Have you ever felt that you were driven in haste and had to go with out the usual process of preparation?

As part of the ritual before the Seder meal, all yeast is ritually cleaned from the house. Even the crumbs are dusted away, lest any odd bit of yeast lay hidden. This yeast now has a symbolic relation to sin. Any ingredients that cause food to rise are seen as representing the ego, or "puffing up" and should be avoided to remain humble. Are there things that cause you to "puff up"? Is your house in need of cleaning to clear away evils that have been allowed to rise? Where are the crumbs hidden?

Once the home is ritually clean, no leavening is to be brought back into the house during the celebration—just as we should not reintroduce bad habits or false teachings back into our lives. If your home is like mine, it takes constant vigilance to keep it clean. And even then things have a way of piling up.

Sacred Seasonings

Notice the warmth of the dough as you knead it. Did that heat surprise you? As you made your flatbread, did you have difficulty making it thin enough? How carefully did you have to watch it on the griddle to keep it from burning? Flatbreads are usually eaten by tearing them apart. Think about the act of tearing. It usually makes us think of something discarded. But what if we are simply sharing with others who have nothing?

As we make and eat our bread, let us remember the simple ingredients that went into this staple of our life. As we share with each other, let us remember to give thanks for what is offered by those around us.

Questions for reflection:

1. What image comes to mind when you think of bread? Do you think of bread as filling in any way?
2. What ingredients in your life act as yeast and leavening?
3. What do you do to keep your house clean? How long are you able to keep it that way? What exactly keeps being reintroduced into your life that keeps you from humility?
4. Because you don't want to risk any yeast rising, it is advisable to make a new batch of bread each day. Are you willing to do all that extra work?

Dear Lord, you know the hidden parts of my life. Help me to search out each crumb and rid my house of evil in your eyes. Make known to me the ways I may be more humble. Give me the strength to share more of myself. Amen.

> There are people in the world so hungry, that God cannot appear to them except in the form of bread.
>
> Mahandas Gandhi

Snow Globes

"The earth is the Lord's and everything in it, the world and all who live in it; for he founded it upon the seas and established it upon the waters."

Psalm 24:1-2

Ingredients:

    Small jar
    Objects for inside of globe
    Glitter or fake snow
    Clean, cold water

Glue object to the inside of the lid of the using a hot glue gun. Make sure the glue has a chance to dry completely and set up. Small items could also be built up with floral clay and then glued on. Cover bottom of jar with glitter or other material of your choice. Fill with clean, cold water remembering to leave a small amount of room for the object to disperse some water. (Warm water may turn cloudy.) Screw on lid, gluing around edge to seal. Turn over and watch the snow fall!

    In his infinite wisdom, God made a magical universe filled with sights and sounds that dazzle the eyes and fill our senses with wonder. The planets rotate on a path we cannot control. The seasons change without our input. The weather literally moves with the wind. The sun rises and sets without our doing anything.

Yet we run at break-neck speed and try to do as many things as we possibly can in the time allotted in one day. We rush around from place to place convincing ourselves the more we work, the better we will be. We feel guilty for stopping to rest—even when we know we need to give ourselves time to rejuvenate. Our world seems to be spinning out of control.

Stop! Don't move! Now take a deep breath and exhale slowly. Pick up your snow globe and gently turn it over. Watch the snow falling gently. Concentrate on each flake as it falls through the water. Slowly turn it over again. What did you hear? Nothing? Then listen to the silence. Think about real snow falling outside your home. What does it sound like?

Think about your busy life. What things have you already done today? Do you ever feel like you just want the world to stop spinning for a few minutes so that you can collect yourself? Imagine all the work you have done today. Let those things be each little piece of snow. Turn over your globe and let all of those things fall away. Now think about the long list of things you feel you have yet to accomplish. Turn the globe over again and let them settle.

There are times in the lives of all of us that our world seems out of control. Things look as though they are falling down around us. We wish we could just gather up the pieces and move on. But looking into your globe you may realize you can't gather up all the pieces. There may be too many of them or they are too widely scattered. Or perhaps you understand there are times when we just have to let things lie where they landed. Look where your snow landed. How has it changed the scene inside the globe?

How many times we wish for our own little world where no one could bother us. It would be peaceful and quiet. Time would seem to stand still. Look around this room. What do you see? Does time seem to be racing by, or are you "in" this moment?

Solitude is a difficult thing for many of us. For whatever reason, we find it difficult to sit quietly alone. Imagine yourself inside your globe. What are you doing? Can you enjoy just being there? Listen! In the silence and peace you might be able to hear the voice of God.

Sacred Seasonings

Maybe it is has been there all the time, but you have been too busy to notice it. Now is your chance to spend some time with Him. What is he saying to you?

The world in which we live is filled with simple and abundant joys that we only need to look upon to notice. Our lives are busy and brimming with tasks to complete and voices to answer. We often complain about the lack of time we have each day, yet we don't take the time offered to us by the one who created us. Spend some time in solitude with God. Let your worries fall down around you and listen to the silence.

Questions for reflection:

1.   Does the snow in your globe land on the object you placed inside? Do you feel like you need to get it off or does it add a new dimension of beauty?
2.   When you shake your globe, the water become bubbly and the snow swirls around. If your feeling "all shook up", how can you settle yourself again?
3.   How do you listen to silence? Is it easy for you? What does it sound like? Do you have to go someplace to be in solitude or is it possible to find a moment wherever you are?
4.   What things are keeping you from hearing the voice of God?

Almighty God, who has given us this wonderful world, help us to see the simple and abundant joys that lie around us. Help us to stop in the midst of our fast-paced life and listen to you. May we not be afraid of the solitude and silence you offer in the comfort of your presence. Amen.

The more faithfully you listen to the voices within you, the better you will hear what is sounding outside.

Dag Hammarskjol

Rain Sticks

"In the past, he let all nations go their own way. Yet he has not left himself without testimony: he has shown kindness by giving you rain from heaven and crops in their seasons; he provides you with plenty of food and fills your hearts with joy."

Acts 14:16-17

Ingredients:

    Paper towel tube
    Straight pins
    White note card or heavy card stock
    Masking tape or clear packing tape
    Rice, beans, pasta, popcorn, etc.

Mark along the rib of the paper towel tube in approximate 1 inch markings. (Following the spiral.) At each mark, insert a straight pin. Tape over the pins to keep them in place. Cut two circles slightly larger than the diameter of the end of the tube from the card stock. Tape one circle to cover the end of the tube. Pour in approximately 1/4 cup various types of beans and pasta. Cover remaining end of cube with the other circle of card stock. The outside of the stick can now be decorated as you please.

Slowly turn stick over and hear the rain fall.

Slowly the drops start falling. Hesitantly they hit the sidewalk. People who are walking start covering their heads and running toward shelter. Cars begin turning on their windshield wipers. There is a steady rhythm of sounds mingling together; raindrops falling and the beating of the wipers back and forth.

We all know water in the form of rain is needed to sustain life on this planet. It is a natural cycle, a rhythm in our lives most of us give only a passing thought. Yet, as weather patterns change, we check the local forecasts and listen intently so that we may plan our activities accordingly. We worry about the possibility of thunderstorms while understanding the dangers of drought.

Those of us in the Midwest are taught about the dustbowl era of the 1930's. We all have seen pictures of scorched desert and barren earth in east Africa. We recognize the devastation caused by the lack of water. We think we can comprehend what it is like to be thirsty. But have you really ever been without water? Have you longed for something, anything to relieve a throat so parched you can't swallow? Can you imagine what it was like to hang on a cross in the hot sun and say, "I thirst"?

Just as we learn about the effects of drought, we are also aware of the results of severe storms. Again, those of us in the Midwest are taught what to do when a tornado is sighted. We learn to shield ourselves from hail or damaging winds. Yet, have you ever considered these very storms were carried here by the wind? The same winds that bring cool breezes can gather speed and force and cause destruction.

The same can be applies to our Christian lives. We feel the presence of God and we feel refreshed, renewed. Then we allow our humanness to fill up the sacred spaces with busyness. The busier we become, our minds become more "clouded". Our outlooks seem to be "drearier". Our relationships become "stormier". Just as the air pressure builds up, stress builds and soon we explode like the atmospheric explosions taking place in thunderclouds. When lightening flashes are discharged between the clouds and the ground, tremendous energy is released. Unless an object is a good conductor of electricity, it will be shattered or set on fire when hit by lightening.

Sacred Seasonings

The tempest building in our souls is not gentle and sometimes damages anything in its path. Haven't we all witnessed hurtful words spark an already charged situation during an angry quarrel?

We try to find balance. Between the times the rain falls, we need sunshine. Just as a seed needs both rain and sunlight to grow, so do we. As much as we want to stay in the sheltering arms of God during the stormy times of our lives, we also need to bask in the *son's* light and grow.

The Bible contains many stories centering around storms. God's almighty force and wrath are seen in Noah and the Great Flood, or Jonah being tossed overboard to calm the waters. The prophets Isaiah and Nahum described God coming in a whirlwind and storms unless the Israelites obeyed the word of God. The image of the frightened disciples, alarmed as the storm tosses their boat while Christ sleeps, remind us all to rely on him and seek his peace. The psalmist speaks of God refreshing the land with rain and God himself being like showers watering the earth. Ezekiel says, God will send us "showers of blessings". How wonderful!

Listen to the sound of the rain as you turn your rain stick over. Does it sound like rushing water or tranquil drops? How is the sound of your stick different from the person's sitting next to you? Try starting with one person and then adding another and another until everyone is in the midst of a rain storm. Is the sound of rain soothing or worrisome? How hard was it to hear anything except the "rain"? Do you think you would be able to hear God in the midst of a storm?

"Boy, we sure do need rain." "The ballgame has been cancelled." "It is so dark and dreary." "But we were going on a picnic!" "The flowers look so much better now that the rain has finally come." "I love to curl up with a good book and listen to the sound of the rain ..." What is your response to a forecast of rain?

Questions for reflection:

1. Do you always listen to the weather report? Why? Must you always be prepared for the worst? Do storms in general frighten you? Why or why not?

Sherri Purdom

2. Have you ever known a time when water was a precious commodity? Did that change your perception of a "natural resource"? How do you carry that memory as a reminder today?

3. What is the most recent "storm on the sea of your soul"? How did it pass? Were you rescued or did you simply ride the storm out?

4. Describe your feelings while you are in "the quiet before a storm". Whose voice do you listen for during a cloudburst?

5. Discuss your favorite Bible story involving storms. What about it speaks to you? Do you recall this story when you are faced with the turbulent times in your life?

6. Do you let rain-or even the threat of rain-"ruin" your plans? Has there ever been a time when a rain shower added to the experience?

Gracious Father in Heaven, give us sunshine and rain so that we may grow. Help us to weather the storms of our own making. Bring us your gentle rains of comfort when we are feeling parched and dry. May we see the nature of your kindness in each day and thank you for our abundance. Amen.

The wise man in the storm prays to God, not from safety from danger, but for deliverance from fear.
                                        Ralph Waldo Emerson

Peanut Butter and Honey Bees

"How sweet are your words to my taste, sweeter than honey to my mouth."

Psalm 119:113

Ingredients:

    1/2 cup peanut butter
    1/2 cup powdered sugar
    1/2 cup honey
    1 1/2 cups graham cracker crumbs (about 12 whole crackers)
    1 square semisweet chocolate or 1 ounce chocolate chips
    1/3 cup sliced almonds. Toasted.

Place a sheet of waxed paper on a cookie sheet so bees won't stick. Combine peanut butter, powdered sugar, and honey in a medium bowl. Stir until mixed well. Stir in graham cracker crumbs. Using hands, shape mixture into 1 1/4 inch ovals. Place on waxed paper. Put chocolate in a small Ziploc bag inside a microwave safe cup or small bowl and microwave on high 1 minute or until melted. Cut out a tiny hole in the corner of the bag. Pipe 3 stripes on each bee. Insert 2 almond slivers in each bee for wings. Use a toothpick or skewer to poke small indentations at one end for eyes. Refrigerate for about an hour. Bees should feel firm when touched. To store, place in tightly covered container in refrigerator.

Everyone has seen a bee hovering over a flower blossom. Maybe it was just a patch of clover, but you saw the bee nevertheless. If you are allergic to bee stings, you might have felt a slight wave of fear. A tiny insect going about her work gathering nectar to take back to the hive to be converted into honey.

We give bees the image of being tireless workers. They are always "busy". The image is not far from the truth. About one-third of the human diet is derived from insect-pollinated plants, and honey bees are responsible for 80 percent of this pollination. Bees are the only insects that make food for human consumption. Honeybees may travel as far as 40,000 miles and visit more than 2 million flowers to gather enough nectar to make one pound of honey. They may be very far from home when you see them in your yard. A single bee will only make one-half teaspoon of honey. Now that's a lot of hard work! Would you be willing to work that hard for such a small outcome?

Yet the outcome of that work is a golden liquid that has had a place in history for 150 million years. Man has been collecting honey for at least 9,000 years. Along with being a sweetening agent, it has been used in cosmetics, as a preservative for fruits, and a healing agent for sore throats. The Romans used honey instead of gold as a means of paying tax. In Germany, peasants were required to give their feudal lords a payment of honey and beeswax.

Honey has long been associated with the sacred. The Greeks offered honey to the gods and spirits of their dead. They created an alcoholic beverage called mead and it was considered the drink of the gods. Egyptians fed honey to their sacred animals. And the Lord told Moses the Promised Land was "flowing with milk and honey".

Let's look at the bee again. This is a small insect that works to produce a minute amount of a substance that is associated with the land of God. In your daily work, do you produce something that can be associated with God?

We often forget how powerful small things can be. Consider words for example. Words can be sweet, even "dripping with honey". They can soothe. They can heal. But words can also be stinging and hurtful. Just like the bee, words are small things that carry both pleasure and pain. Do you pay attention to the type of words you use? Are your words pleasant or painful?

Remember Winnie the Pooh? Here was a little bear who never said bad things about anyone else and was always looking for "just a spot of honey". What about God's words? Do you constantly seek them? Doesn't God want us to speak in love with each other? Perhaps, just a spot of God's words will do the trick and satisfy us simply and fully.

Questions for reflection:

1. How far would you travel to do God's work? Have you ever felt like your obligations to your faith were just "busy work"?
2. What sweet thing do you associate with the sacred? Is it something you produce or gather?
3. As you go about your daily work, are you mindful of the work you do for God? What little thing have you done this week that may have seemed insignificant if only viewed as a single act?
4. When was the last time you felt stung by someone's words or actions? Did you look for healing, or did you strike back? How did you soothe your wounds?
5. Do you speak differently to different people? Why? How does God speak to you? Do you think he speaks the same way to everyone?

God, you provide such sweetness for us. Help us to make ourselves busy doing your work rather than our own. Keep us mindful of the words we speak. May we continue to search for your words that will satisfy our hunger for you. Amen.

> Labor, even the most humble and the most obscure, if it is well done, tends to beautify and embellish the world.
>
> Gabriele D'Annunzio

Pretzels

"You will call upon me and come and pray to me, and I will listen to you. You will seek me and find me when you seek me with all your heart."
Jeremiah 29:12-13

Ingredients:

1 package active dry yeast
1/8 cup warm water (105 degrees)
1 1/3 cup warm water
1/3 cup brown sugar
5 cups flour
2 tablespoons baking soda per 1 cup water

Dissolve yeast in the 1/8 cup 105 degree water. Stir in other 1 1/3 cups warm water. Add the brown sugar and flour. Beat until smooth. Knead dough lightly on floured surface until smooth and elastic. Heat oven to 475 degrees. Fill a saucepan with 2 tablespoons baking soda per every one cup of water until full. Boil baking soda and water. Tear off some dough and roll a pencil shape with your hands. Pick it up gently by both ends, cross to form rabbit ears, then twist the ends around again and pull them back down toward you to rest on the loop. Place twisted pretzel in the boiling water for

15 seconds, until pretzel dough is golden or yellow in color. Remove pretzel from water and place onto a lightly salted cookie sheet. Continue until cookie sheet is full. Sprinkle coarse salt on top of pretzels. Place cookie sheet into oven and bake for 8-10 minutes or until pretzels are golden brown.

Pretzels are known to be one of the oldest snack foods. They date back as early as 610 (CE) to a monastery in Southern France or Northern Italy where monks used scraps of dough to form a treat representing a child's arms folded in prayer. These treats were used to bribe the children into memorizing their Bible verses and prayers. The humble enticement grew into a regular request for bakers and eventually spread throughout medieval Europe. In Germany, traveling merchants were in danger of being robbed by bandits. In order to protect the tradesmen, the townspeople would ride out and meet them bringing pitchers of wine and large amounts of crisp dough called Geleit-pretzels.

Pretzels continued to be associated with religion or religious activity. In 1450, Germans had pretzels with hard-boiled eggs nestled in each of the round curves for dinner on Good Friday. The pretzels represented everlasting life and the eggs represented Easter's rebirth.

The term "tying the knot" is thought to have originated with Royal weddings in 1614. The couples would wish for happiness with a pretzel forming the nuptial knot. They would break it much like we pull wishbones for good luck today.

But let's return to the original symbol: arms folded in prayer. In our Western idea of prayer, many of us feel we must sit with our hands clasped and our heads bowed. We sit (or kneel) quietly and often spend a great deal of our time asking God for things or for help.

Prayer is our way of communicating with God. And sometimes, if we wait long enough and listen hard enough, God will communicate with us. Spending time alone with God is often uncomfortable. We aren't sure if we are "doing it right" or what exactly we are supposed to "hear". We forget our prayer time is time to simply have a conversation with God. Children understand this. When left alone, children show us the basic, honest way of communicating— whether with us or with God. The don't hold anything back.

Have you tried praying in different ways? Have you gotten on your knees other places besides an altar railing? Have you ever lifted your arms wide to heaven to feel God's embrace as he whispers lovingly to you? Have you sat with your hands resting open on your lap expectantly?

Sometimes we are afraid of not saying the "right" things in prayer. We try filtering our petitions, as if God won't know what our true needs are. Did you find twisting your pretzel to be difficult? Did you need it to *look* like a pretzel? Although it may not look like you had envisioned it to look, it is still a pretzel. And although you may not actually speak to God about something, he knows what is in your heart.

Boiling the dough before putting it into the oven makes the pretzel soft on the inside. The process of baking it in the oven creates the crunchy exterior. At times I feel like a pretzel. I am vulnerable on the inside, but can have a tough outer exterior. I may be able to prevent some from getting to know what is really going on inside of me, but God sees and hears me all the time. And if we listen, he will speak to us.

As adults, we aren't asked to memorize scripture verses. But have you read a piece of scripture that spoke directly to your heart? Didn't you want to enfold it into your life? It is at these times God is speaking directly to you. The next time that happens, try reciting it aloud while crossing your arms over your chest in the way of the pretzel. Hold it close to your heart and remember God hears all your prayers.

Questions for reflection:

1. How long do you spend in prayer each day? Do you have a special place to spend time with God? Do you feel you can really open your heart to God?
2. Did you pray as a child? What type of prayers did you have? Were they only said at certain times or in certain ways? What type of prayers do you have now?
3. What types of things "tie you up in knots"? When you are feeling this way, is it easier or more difficult to pray? Why?

4. Cross your arms over your chest covering your heart. Describe this feeling. Is it awkward? Do you feel protective or defensive? Do you feel you must guard your heart?

God, you are great and oh so good to us! Let us take this time to thank you for our many blessings each day. Thank you for the food we eat and the fellowship we share. Help us to remember you not only hear our pleas, our wants; but you also rejoice with us and want us to open our hearts to you. Amen.

When you pray, rather let your heart be without words than your words without heart.

John Bunyan

Musical Instruments

"It is good to praise the Lord and make music to your name, O Most High"

Psalm 92:1

Ingredients:

Paper plates
Yarn
Metal washers
Empty cans and jars
Empty oatmeal and tissue boxes
Toilet paper tubes
Rubber bands
Various beans, rice, pasta, etc.
Tissue or waxed paper

- Fill recycled items such as boxes, jars, bottles, or cans with small amounts of beans, rice, pasta, etc. Glue or tape caps or lids shut to make shakers.
- Punch holes around the rim of two paper plates with a hole punch. Put plates facing each other and tie on two metal washers per hole with string or yarn to make tambourine.

- Place rubber bands around the middle of a tissue box stringing them over the open hole. Stoke bands to make sounds. (Twisting each rubber band and tying off at different intervals in the back of the box will produce different pitches with the strings.)
- Tissue paper wrapped around a comb and waxed paper put over the end of toilet paper tube, then secured with a rubber band will make kazoos.
- Place lid on empty oatmeal box and use for a drum.
- Take an empty can and run a stick or utensil across the "ribs" for another rhythm instrument.
- Blow across a bottle to make a flute.
- Rub rims of glasses filled with water at different levels to form a musical scale.

Music is sound that has some degree of rhythm, melody, and harmony. The word instrument literally means a device for producing music. That pretty much covers everything! Babbling brooks, wind rustling the leaves of trees, children laughing-are all instruments of music.

As long as there have been people on this planet, there has been some type of musical instruments. In 1996, archeologists found in a Neanderthal campsite in Slovenia part of a femur bone of a cave bear that had holes bored into it at definite intervals as some sort of flute-type instrument. The spacing of the holes resembles the same type of musical scale we know today. This flute is approximately 40,000-82,000 years old! Other ancient flutes made from hollowed reeds have been found in China and date back 9,000 years.

In early Biblical times, music was functional. It had a purpose. It was used as military signals in battle or in liturgical chants and rituals in the temple. Bells were sewn on the hem of the garments of priests to chase away evil spirits. Music accompanied prophetic declarations. Even in secular or cultic festivals, music was used as a means of distraction and release.

Music as we know it today has many varied uses. It may be use to soothe or calm as with lullabies. A certain song may evoke memories or emotions. Music is used to set the mood. For some, music is used in alternative healing practices to relieve stress and calm the body. There are studies done to see if music heard while in the uterus leads to higher intelligence. We use music to teach concepts to children. And sometimes, music is just nonsense-but it can bring smile to young and old alike.

Even from Biblical times, God filled his servants with such joy, they could do nothing but break into singing and dancing. When Moses led the Israelites across the Red Sea, his sister Miriam took up a tambourine and began singing a song of victory.

Have you ever felt such joy fill your soul you just *had* to sing or dance or make music? Make some music now. Shake, scrape, rattle, bang, blow, drum–make a joyful noise! We try do hard to always be in control We are afraid of looking (or sounding) silly or stupid. Yet, there are times we need to join in merrymaking and express our joy. Make some more music!

At first, the sounds of all our instruments together may not sound like "music". In fact, it might even sound like someone dropped a box of trash! Try playing them one at a time. Go around the room and let everyone demonstrate their own instrument. Now try it again continuing to play as each person joins in one at a time until all are playing. Try it again, this time beating out the rhythm of your name. What happened? Was there laughter? Did you feel silly? Did the group start playing a certain beat or rhythm?

Remember as children when we grabbed the first thing that made a sound and marched around the room wanting everyone to join us? Don't we want to have others join in our fun?

Did you know a "band" is just a group of people joined in common purpose? Look around at this band. For what purpose are joined? Let us praise God with his words. As you go around the room again, one at a time, quote your favorite scripture verse and follow it by playing your instrument. Did your music seem to have a purpose now?

Playing your instrument following a scripture was like adding an exclamation point to the words. That is what God wants us to do. He wants us to hear his words, take them into our hearts and share them with exclamation. Make some music! Let your soul be filled with joy so you can't help but share it.

We spend a great amount of time trying to orchestrate our lives. We think we have control over how and when certain instruments should enter our piece/peace. We think we know just how the melody of our lives should sound, but often a discordant sound appears and makes a new tune. Can you make this a joyful noise? If only we could listen to our souls and follow the rhythm God sets before us. A new song will be created and played for all to hear.

Questions for reflection:

1. How do you use music? Is it utilitarian or just aesthetic? Are there some types of music you only enjoy privately?
2. What types of things fill your soul with joy? How do you express it?
3. Do you consider yourself "musical"? Is it easier to play your instrument alone or with others? What is your favorite instrument? Why?
4. Where in your life do you want to add an "exclamation point"?
5. Do all the different parts of your life come together in harmony? How much control do you have when a new instrument is ready to join your song? What does God's music in your life sound like?

God of laughter, God of music, may we share the joy in our souls with wild abandon. Help us to take up our tambourine and sing our songs of victory we have through you. May we hear the songs of comfort and healing, of lullabies and nonsense, and of joyful noise that you play for us each day. Amen. "Selah"

After silence, that which comes nearest to expressing the inexpressible is music.

Aldous Huxley

Continuing to Feast on the Goodness of the Lord

Small groups are great for exploring new ways to see God in familiar objects. But how do we find these insights in large corporate worship services? Too often we separate our personal moments with God and worshiping in a group setting. It is possible to have both.

Our usual method of worship is a formal service in a sanctuary attended by clergy in robes (or at least a suit and tie). There is a lot to be said for tradition. It connects us to our past and reminds us of where we came. Worship services can bring us into the presence of God with the opening strains of an organ prelude or the music of contemporary praise songs by a band. Perhaps it comes in the singing of the Doxology after the offering plate has been passed.

So often, after becoming familiar with the way a worship service is performed, we forget our purpose for being there in the first place. We come together corporately to spend time with our Creator. We sit in our usual seat and greet the same people every week and become very comfortable with our style of prayer and praise. We become a consumer of the service. We come to be "fed", yet we don't partake. We come to be "uplifted", yet we don't fully participate. Some people who don't attend regularly have said, "It is because I don't get anything out of it." But what have they brought to it? Or what have they put into it?

As we grow in our faith, we better understand our relationship with God. We join in the give and take of dialogue through prayer. We desire to spend time with someone who cares for us. We long to be in the presence of a Living God. In searching for this place, we must be aware and open our senses to him as we participate in the familiar rituals of worship.

The easiest way we sense him is through listening. We listen to sermons, music, and prayers. We try to be good listeners to friends and colleagues. Some even say they spend time listening for the voice of God. But we often forget to listen to silence. We ignore the voices of nature. We listen with our ears, but not always with our hearts.

Listening is not really a passive act. It requires us to think about what we are hearing and process it. People are so afraid of taking the time to listen. Fear of being challenged or fear of being called on later keeps some people only half listening. Maybe it is a fear of feeling an emotion they don't want to deal with that keeps them at arms length away. Instead of waiting for an answer to prayer, we are busy asking God for something else. Do we think God is always going to tell us "no"? Maybe he will, but if we don't wait for the answer, how do we know? Half listening also means our mouths are probably engaged too soon after the words enter the ear canals.

Take a few minutes. Digest the meat of the message. What exactly is the meat of the message? Can you relate it in some way to your life, some experience you have had in the past week? Is there something said that will echo in you as you continue with your life this next week? Let the words or music or silence wash over you. Let it stir images or memories. Let sound resonate within all of your body and let it connect within you to your soul so that you do hear God. Listen to the choir of angels. Do they sound like a 50 voice group of trained voices with trumpets and timpani? Or does it sound more like a shy group of a dozen 4 and 5 year olds singing with innocence and abandon? When you are responding to the liturgy, are you really listening to the words you are saying? Is this a creed you believe? Is this a prayer from your heart or only words on a bulletin? Listen for the sound of footsteps. Hear Christ walking

Sacred Seasonings

beside you as you walk a prayer trail in the woods or walk down the carpeted aisle of a sanctuary?

I am a visual learner. I like pictures that I can translate into a personal experience. My mother and I have what we call "Show and Tell" each time we visit each other. We come armed with a tote bag of newspaper clippings, magazine articles, kid's drawings, programs, bulletins, recipes, and various other assundry items that we just had to share with the other. We could just talk about all of these things, but actually seeing them brings them life and enhances what ever story we are telling.

The same is true for the worship experience. A lit candle is a tangible visual stimulus reminding me the Holy Spirit is present at that gathering. A basket of canned goods gathered for the needy in the community and placed at the foot of the altar is a reminder of my abundant bounty and how blessed I can be in sharing what I have with others. A Chrismon Tree during Advent connects me not only to the season at hand, but also the life of Christ depicted in the symbols hanging on the tree and to the hands that lovingly created those ornaments. Let your eyes wander and see all the things you have seen before, and yet never have really noticed.

I love going into different churches because I enjoy seeing where they have placed the cross. Enjoy the beauty of various altars and the items upon it. I appreciate the sacredness of icons and statuary in Orthodox and Catholic churches. While I may not understand the specific symbolism in a particular stained glass window, I let it speak to me in color, shape, and the scene depicted. I delight in the sun dancing through the window and landing on the face of the person sitting in front of me. The brilliance of poinsettias at Christmas and bright white of the lilies at Easter fill my eyes and touch me in a place that remembers Christmas' and Easters' past. Have you really looked at the people holding candles during a candlelight service? Do you see how the glow of the candle makes a halo effect around a person's face? See how carefully we all hold the candles so no wax drips? What would the world be like if we cared for each other that way and held each other tightly, yet gently, cradling the fragile light easily extinguished by a small breeze?

Those of us in the Protestant tradition don't get a lot of chances to use our sense of smell during a worship service. Incense is not something we associate with worship. But other faiths do. It is another tangible way of remembering the presence of God and the honor we give him. It can also help us visualize our prayers rising to God as we see the smoke from the censor rise upward. Infrequently, we may have the opportunity to smell oil. The rich heady smell of myrrh can fill our senses and remind us of the richness of kings. Let it remind you how the King of Kings was born in a lowly stable. Have you participated in a living Christmas pageant? Have you ever been around farm animals? The smells of sheep and cattle are not ones you can forget. Yet we certainly don't associate them with worshiping our God. We forget so easily how both the smell of perfume and animals were present at the birth of our Savior. The two smells together: animals and gifts for the King. And later, myrrh was brought to be placed on the body of Christ as he was taken down from the cross. The same smell at very different times in the life of our Lord.

We all do experience a time of celebrating the Lord's Supper. Unfortunately, we become so methodical in our partaking of the bread and wine. The next time you go forward, try to smell the bread. There are few things that compare to the smell of fresh bread recently broken. Smell the wine (or grape juice). Remember the bitter tears shed when Christ died on the cross. Let smell envelope you. I like scented candles just for that reason: they fill the room not only with light, but also with fragrance.

Our sense of taste is interwoven with our senses of smell and sight. When we see a rich dessert our mouths start to salivate with anticipation. Why isn't the same true with Communion? We the see the bread. Perhaps we smell the freshness of it. Do we savor the taste? Are we anxious to come into the presence of our Lord? Or is this yet another ritual we mindlessly walk toward while we notice how late the service is running?

Mealtimes are at once sacred and human. They are a time of coming together as a family. They are a time of fellowship among friends, of just enjoying another's company. How sad we don't always come to God's table with that same attitude. We come bringing him our problems and concerns. We come because it is a ritual. We come because that is a part of" being a Christian". Come and be fed! Come and enjoy the company of the Lord! Come and join in a feast! Come and commune together. As you taste the holy elements, taste the love God has for you.

And the next time you are invited to a pot luck dinner in the church basement, remember Christ wanted us to dine together. Taste the love each cook has brought in their dish. Thank God for a chance to have fellowship and enjoy each other's company.

Christian churches all contain some type of cross in their sanctuaries. Some are brass, some are smooth pine, and others are rough lumber. Have you ever reached out and touched a cross? What does it feel like? Have you closed your eyes and held a nail? Can you feel the sharp point and the coldness of the metal? What is the weight of such an image of death?

When you kneel at the altar, do you feel what is under your knees? Is it wood or soft velvet cushions? Some churches have hand-sewn kneeling pads done in needlework. When you kneel at the altar, do you think of the women of the church who spent countless hours creating the work of art in a kneeling pad?

Feel the hand of the person sitting next to you in the pew. Is it weathered with age, or tender as a child's? Feel the arms of a friend around you as you pass the peace of Christ. Close your eyes and feel your own body. Are you sitting in excited anticipation? Do you feel relaxed or are you apprehensive about what you may be asked to do next? Concentrate on your breathing. Feel your chest rise and fall.

When does what you physically touch become a "feeling"? Can touching something with your hand evoke a response deep inside of you? Are you moved to tears? What does *that* feel like? Don't worry about what other people might be thinking about you. This is your time. You have permission to experience this sense of touch and emotion. When was the last time you said you were "touched by" some music, or a thoughtful gesture, or a particular scripture verse?

For many of us, looking at our spirituality is scary enough on its own. We may be very uncomfortable trying new things. The rituals and familiarity are safe and secure. We know God's word won't change and we are content to continue the way we always have. I'm not suggesting we all abandon those things we hold dear. There are particular parts of worship I look forward to because I know I will always see God there. I am simply asking you to try expanding your perspective. You may be pleasantly surprised at the old and new friends you will meet along the way. Just open your senses and be ready for the Lord to speak to you.

Seeing our Father in everything makes life one long thanksgiving and gives rest of the heart.

Hannah Whithall Smith

Printed in the United States
1375100006B/166-267